LAGRANGE COUNTY PUBLIC LIBRARY
LGR   j NIE 121966
Nielsen   Telling the truth

3 0477 0002 8543 1

OFFICIAL DISCARD
LaGrange County Public Library

Telling the Truth

by Shelly Nielsen
illustrated by
Virginia Kylberg

Published by Abdo & Daughters, 6535 Cecilia Circle, Edina, Minnesota 55439

Copyright© 1992 by Abdo Consulting Group, Inc., Pentagon Tower, P.O. Box 36036, Minneapolis, Minnesota 55435. International copyrights reserved in all countries. No part of this book may be reproduced in any form without written permission from the publisher. Printed in the United States.

Edited by: Rosemary Wallner

Library of Congress Cataloging-in-Publication Data

Nielsen, Shelly, 1958-
    Telling the Truth / written by Shelly Nielsen ; edited by Rosemary Wallner.
        p. cm. -- (Values matter)
    Summary: Poems present situations when telling the truth is important.
    ISBN 1-56239-062-7
    1. Truthfulness and falsehood -- Juvenile poetry. 2. Children's poetry, American.
[1. Honesty -- Poetry. 2. Conduct of life – Poetry. 3. American poetry.]
I. Wallner, Rosemary, 1964-   . II. Title. III. Series: Nielsen, Shelly, 1958-
Values matter.
PS3564.I354T45 1992   811'.54--dc20   91-73046
                                                                                    CIP
                                                                                    AC

Telling the Truth

Abdo & Daughters
Minneapolis

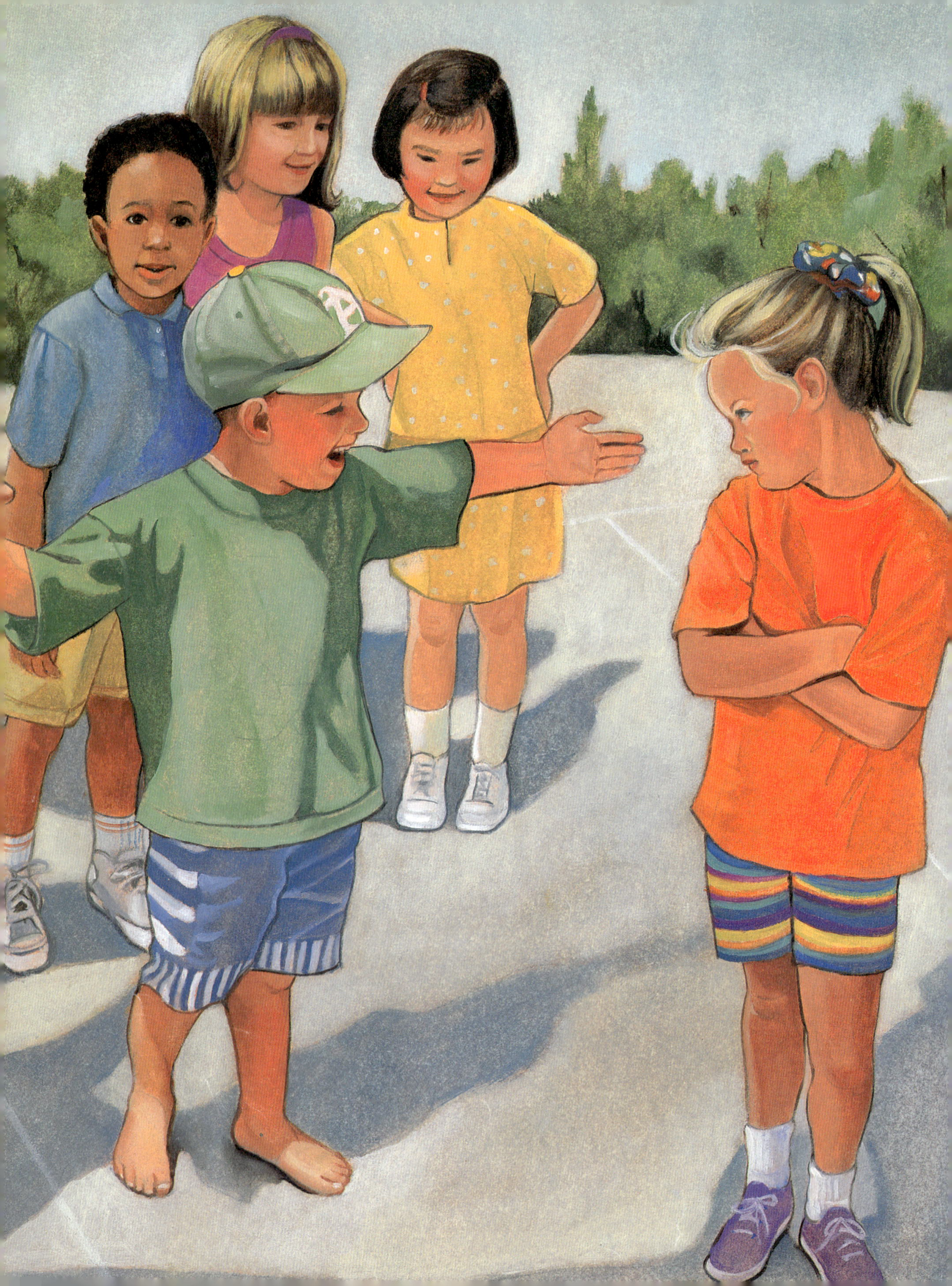

What's a Lie?

A fib,
a lie,
a tale,
a whopper.
No matter what
you call it,
stop it!
Whether it's told
by me or you,
a lie is
never,
ever
true.

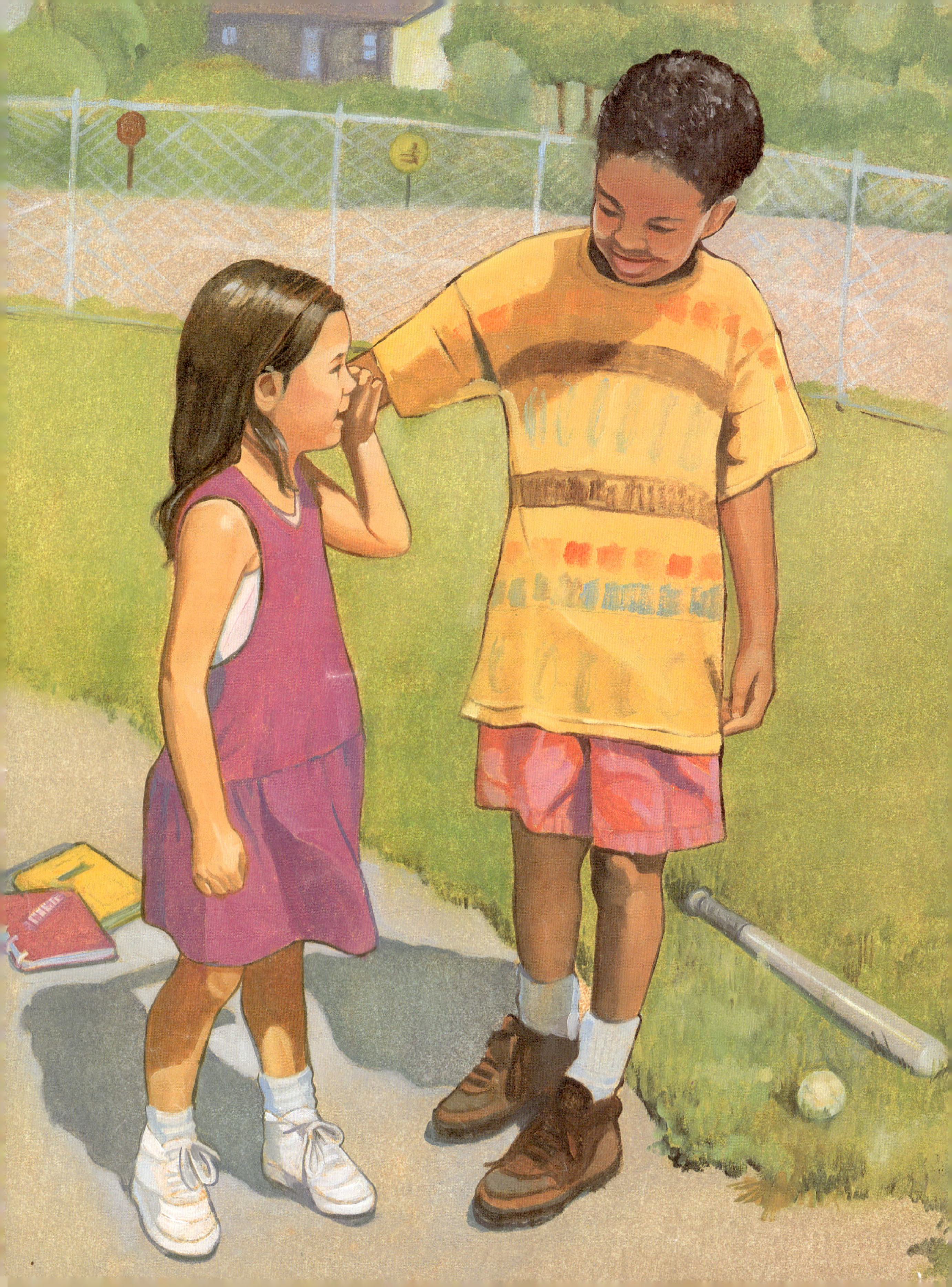

Lies Hurt!

I said Kerry had cooties.
I knew it wasn't true.
Kerry cried, she felt so bad,
so here's what I had to do:
    "I'm sorry, Kerry.
      I shouldn't have lied."
We *both* felt better
when I'd made things right.

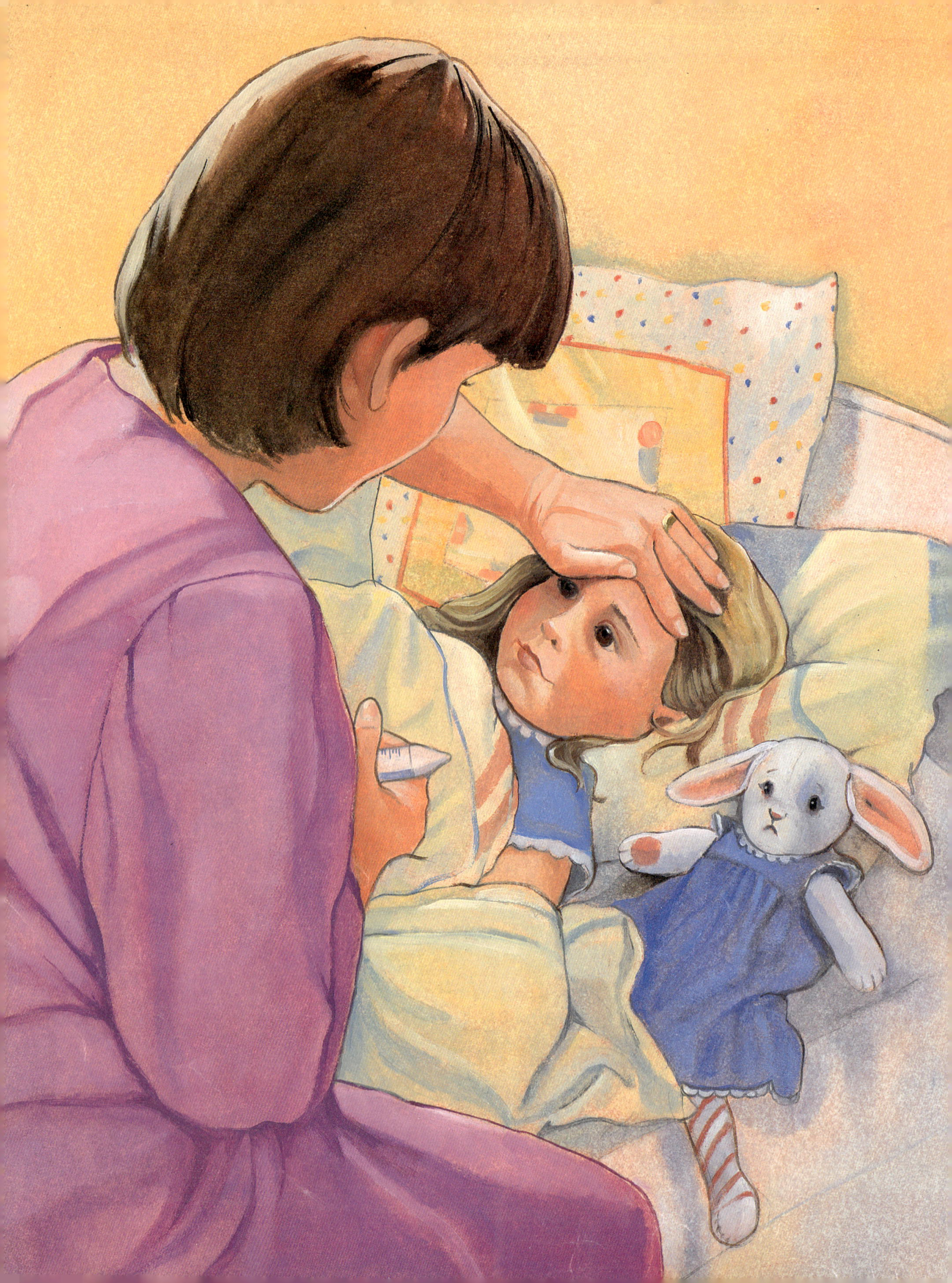

A-Choo!

A made-up ache.
A phoney groan.
A pretend sneeze.
A fake moan.
Acting sick
isn't easy to do
when I can't remember
if I have a cold or the flu!
So I don't pretend,
I don't fake.
I wait till I'm sick
to cough and ache.

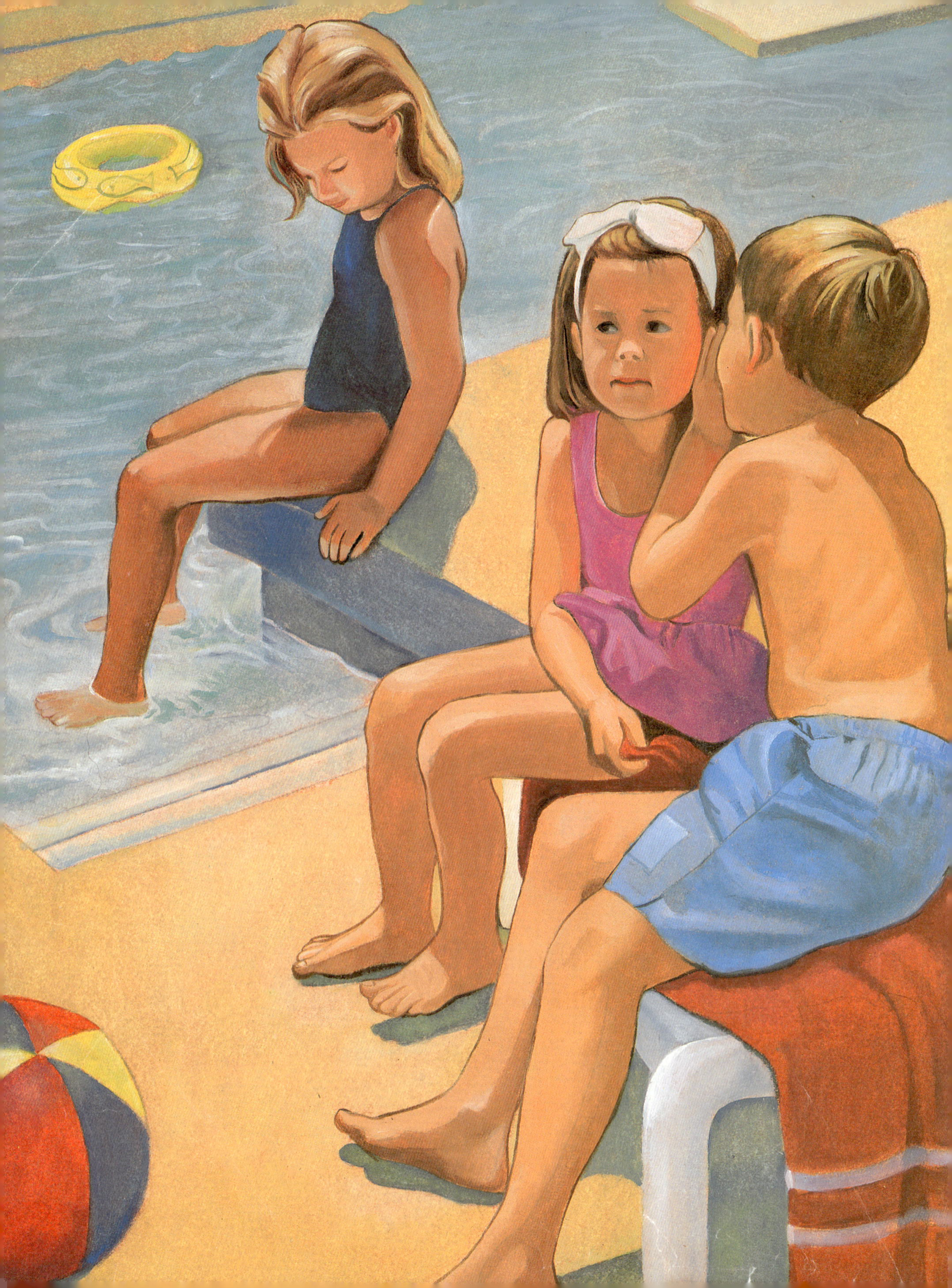

The Pretend Friend

Corey told Kristin
and Kristin told me
that Stephanie doesn't like me.
She was only being nice at school
so she could play
in my swimming pool.
That means
it was all pretend!
There's nothing worse
than a phoney friend.

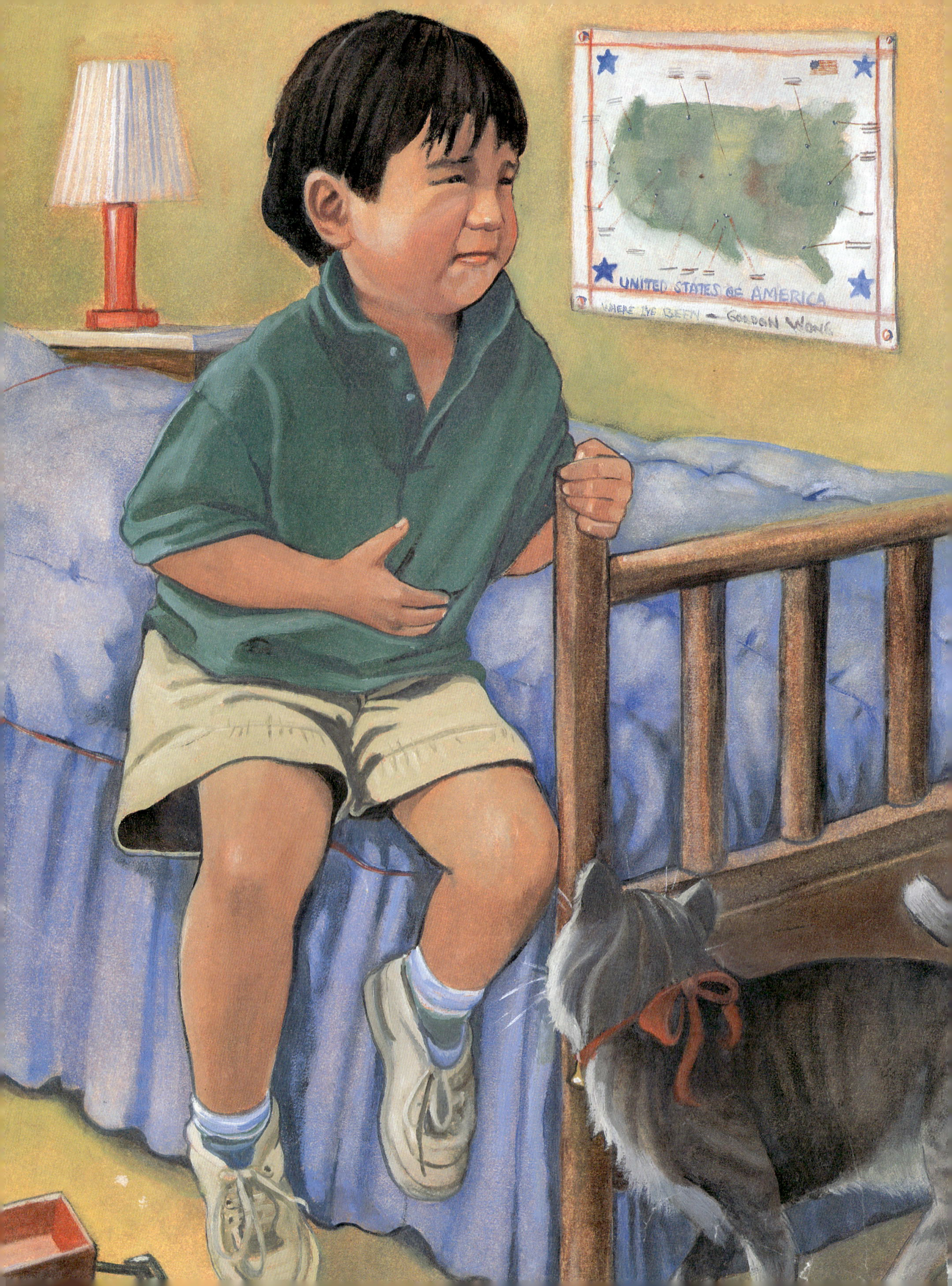
UNITED STATES OF AMERICA
WHERE I'VE BEEN — GORDON WONG

Yesterday's Lie

I told a lie yesterday...
so why does my stomach
hurt today?
I'd like to forget it,
just go out and play;
but lies always make
my stomach ache.

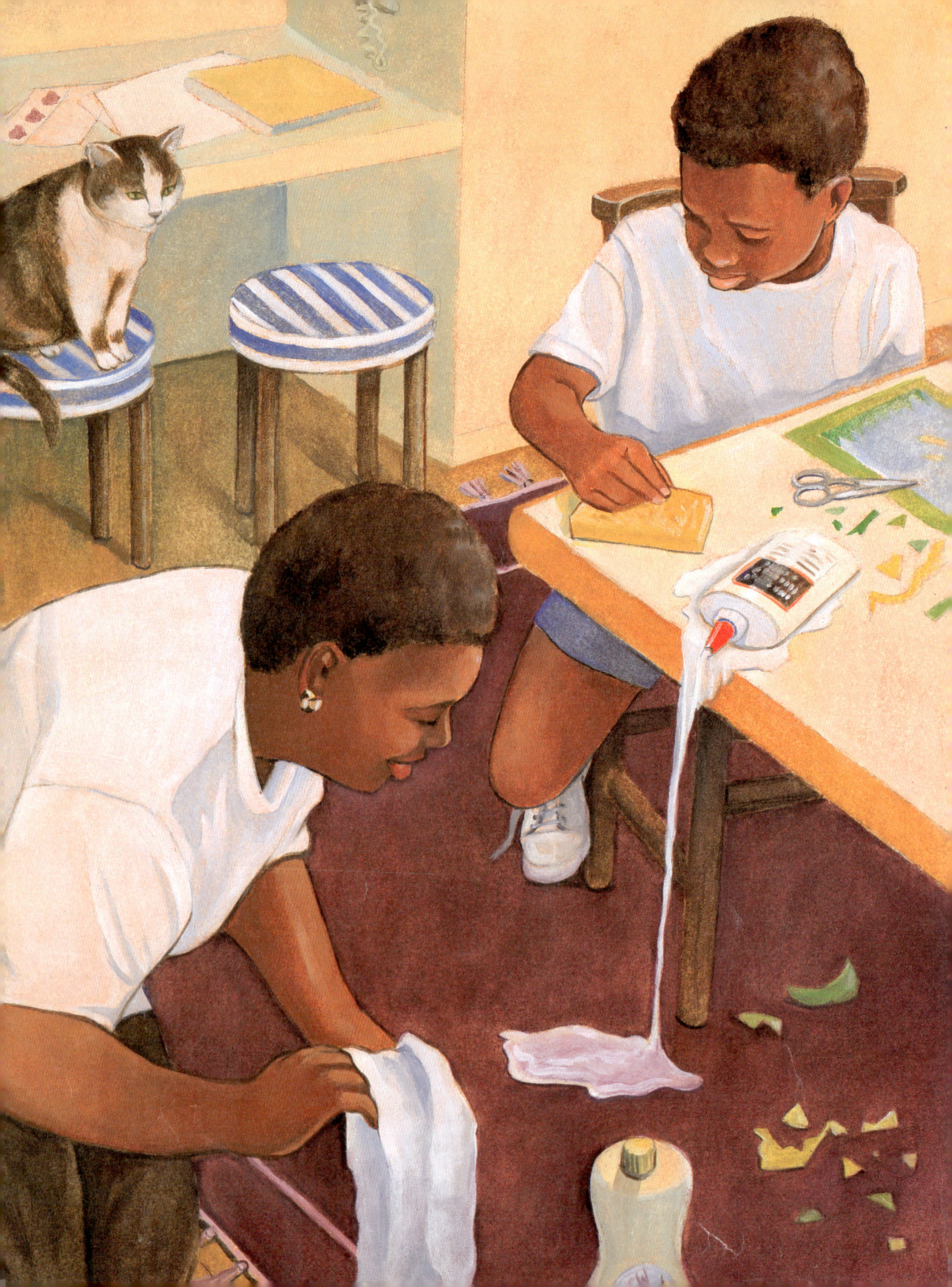

Scared to Tell

Oh-oh!
I spilled
sticky, oozy, gooey glue
all over our carpeting that's brand new.
It's on the table,
all over the floor —
half a bottle, maybe more.

I'd like to run
or disappear
or maybe leave town
for a thousand years.
But...
instead, I say,
"Mom, I dumped the glue.
I really didn't mean to."

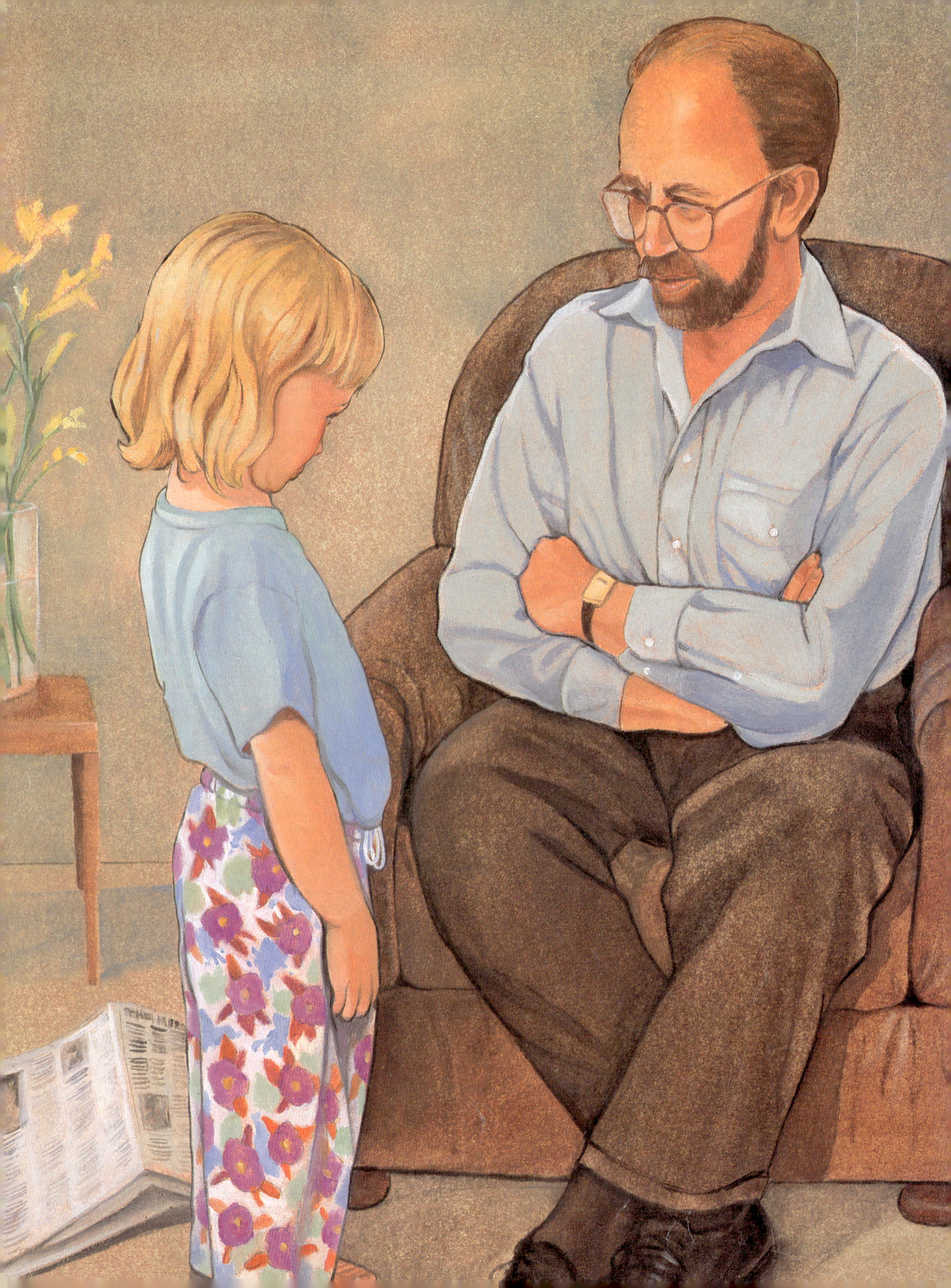

Dad Can Tell

I don't know how,
I don't know why...
Dad can see when I'm telling a lie.
    It's such a pain,
    it's such a disgrace,
    to have lies written
    all over my face.

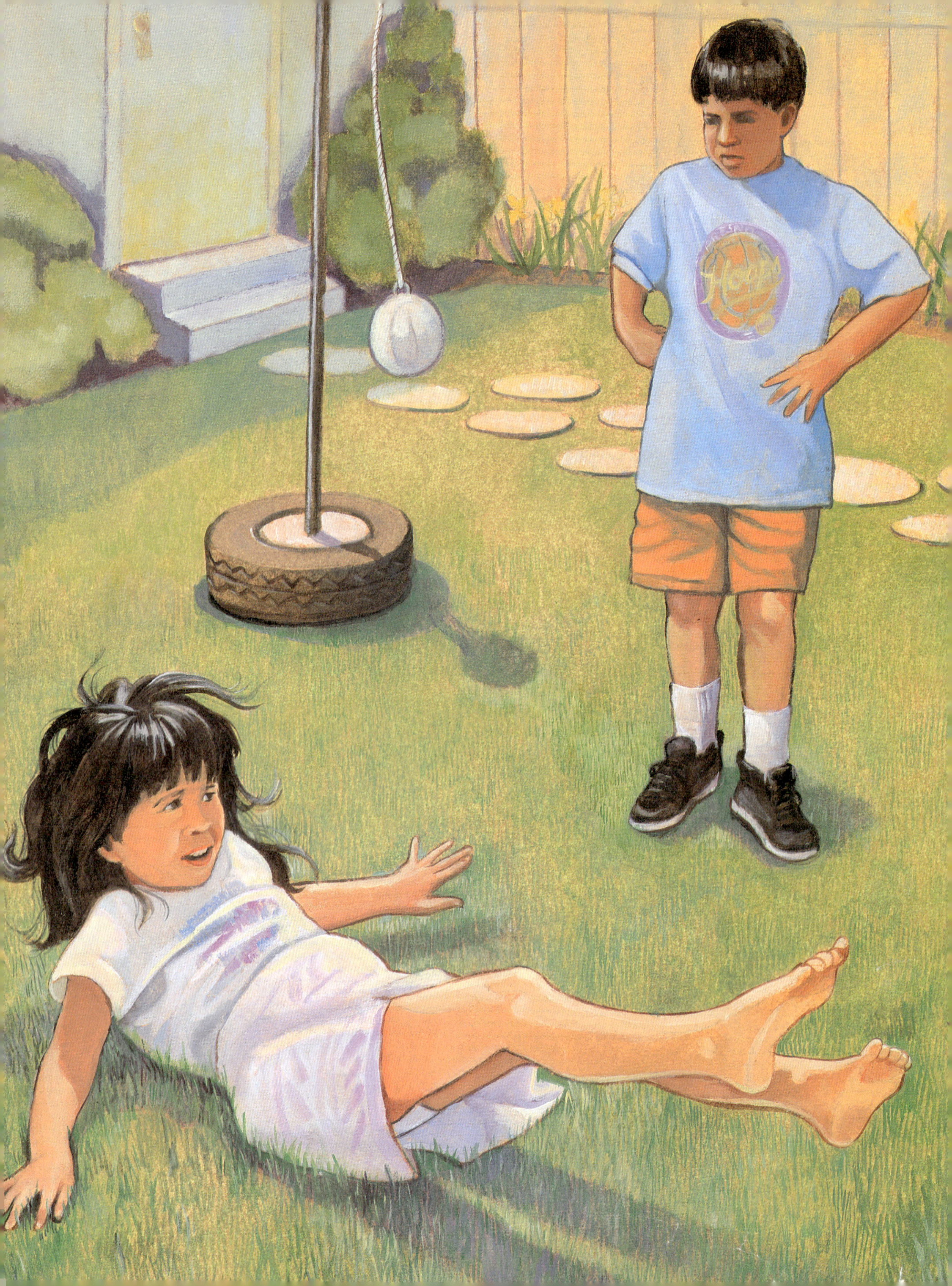

Brag, Brag, Brag

HEY, BRANDON,
LOOK AT ME.
I'M THE BEST CARTWHEELER
THAT WILL EVER BE.
JUST STAND BACK!
WATCH ME JUMP!
HERE I GO!
WHOOPS! KA-WHUMP!
    Well...
    er...
    um...
    Did I say I was the *greatest* in creation?
    Pardon my exaggeration.

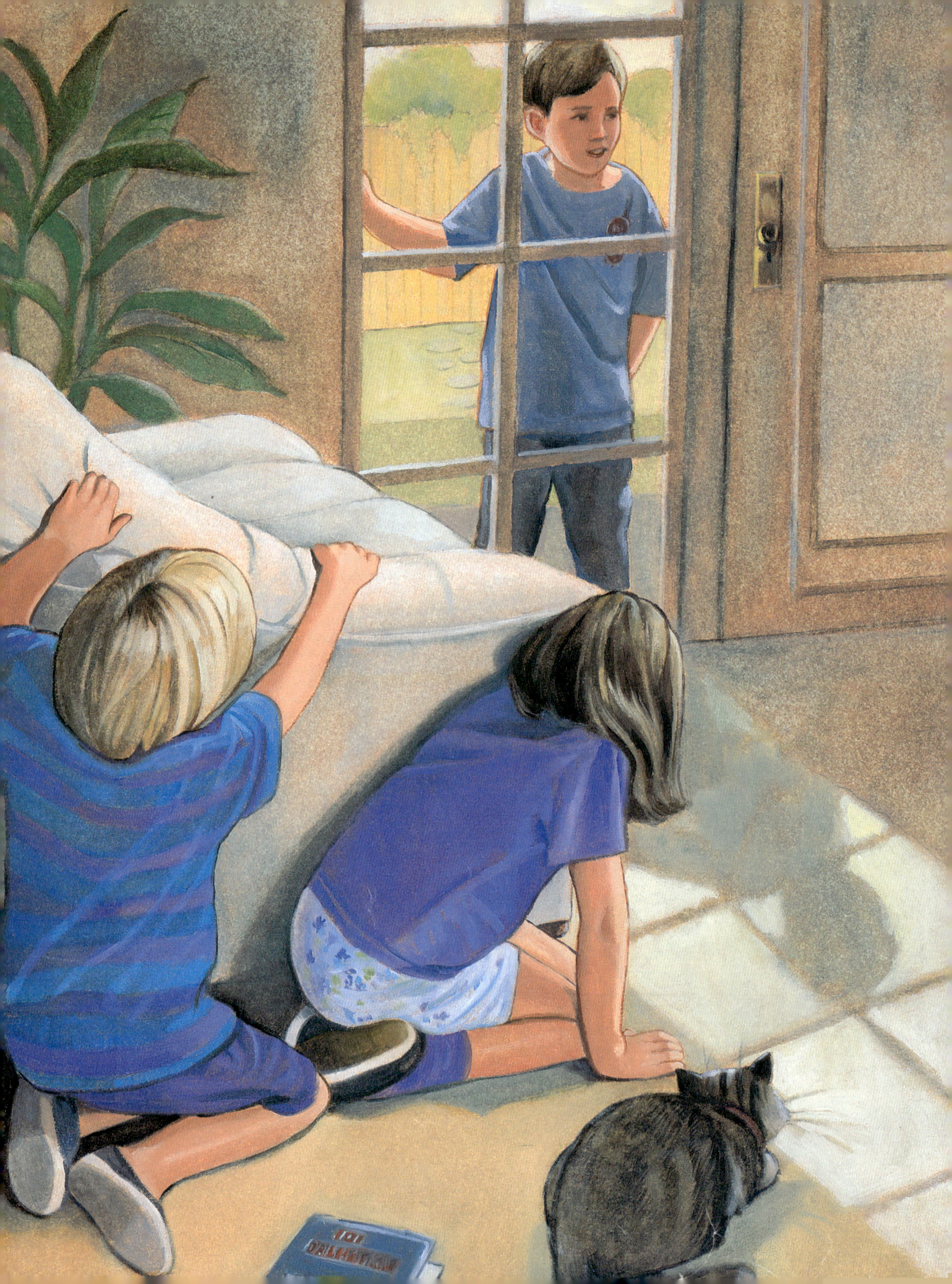

Anybody Home?

Hide!
Here he comes!
Whenever Ron appears,
we run.
DING-DONG!
He's at the door.
We hide and pretend
we're not at home.
Can he hear us giggle?
Did he see us running?
If he knew we were hiding,
would he feel funny?

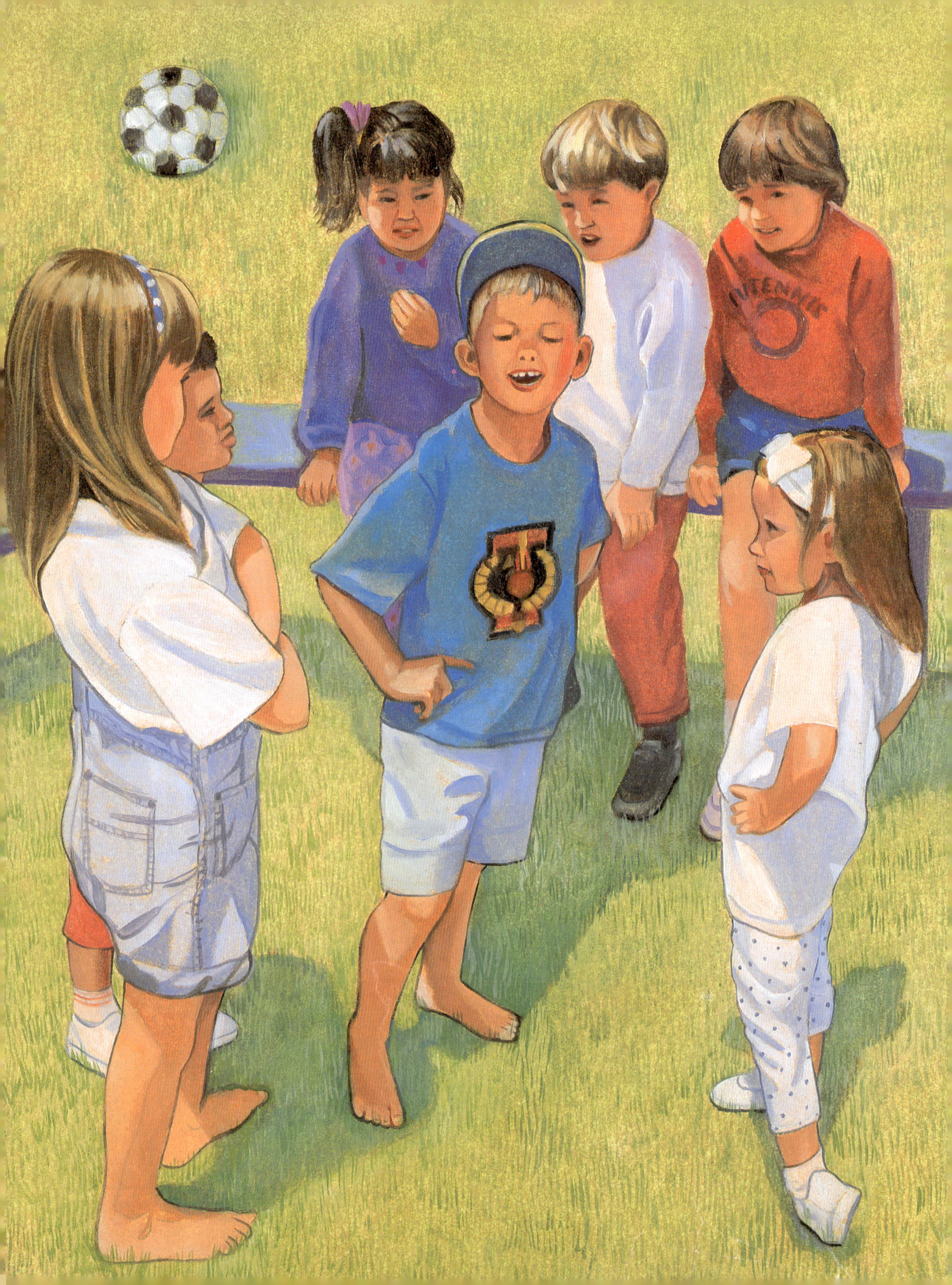

Puffed Up

That Joey acts like he's the King of Siam.
He marches around
like he owns the land.
He says, "You know, I'm very rich,"
until we all feel green and sick.
I wish Joey would just be nice
and stop telling puffed-up lies.

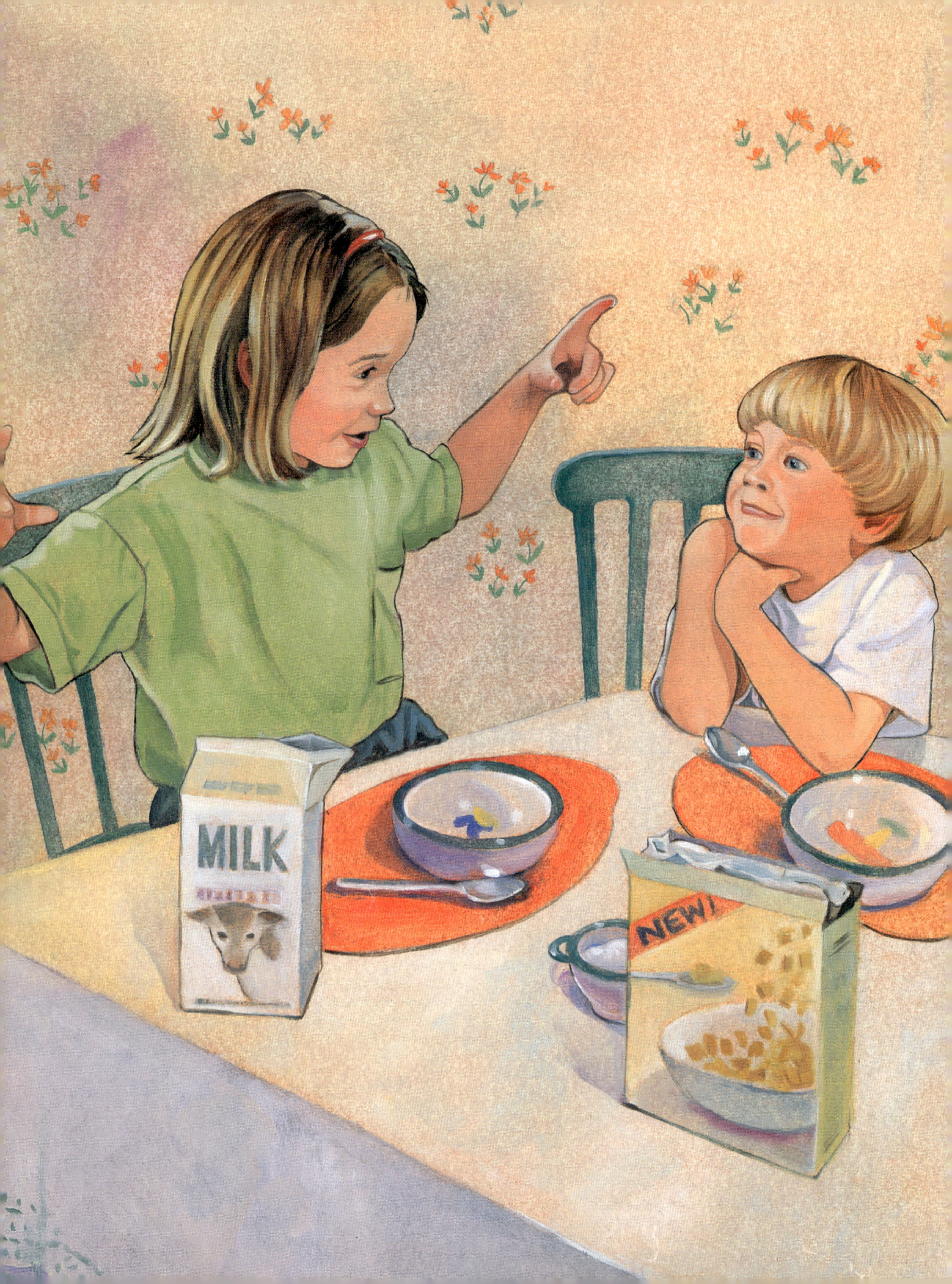
MILK
NEW!

Little White Lies

Little white lies
sound so sweet
You could sprinkle them with sugar
and gladly eat 'em.
You could shish kebab 'em
or put 'em in a bowl,
dump on milk,
and swallow them whole.
But as soon as lies
are in my mouth,
they don't taste sweet,
they turn sour!

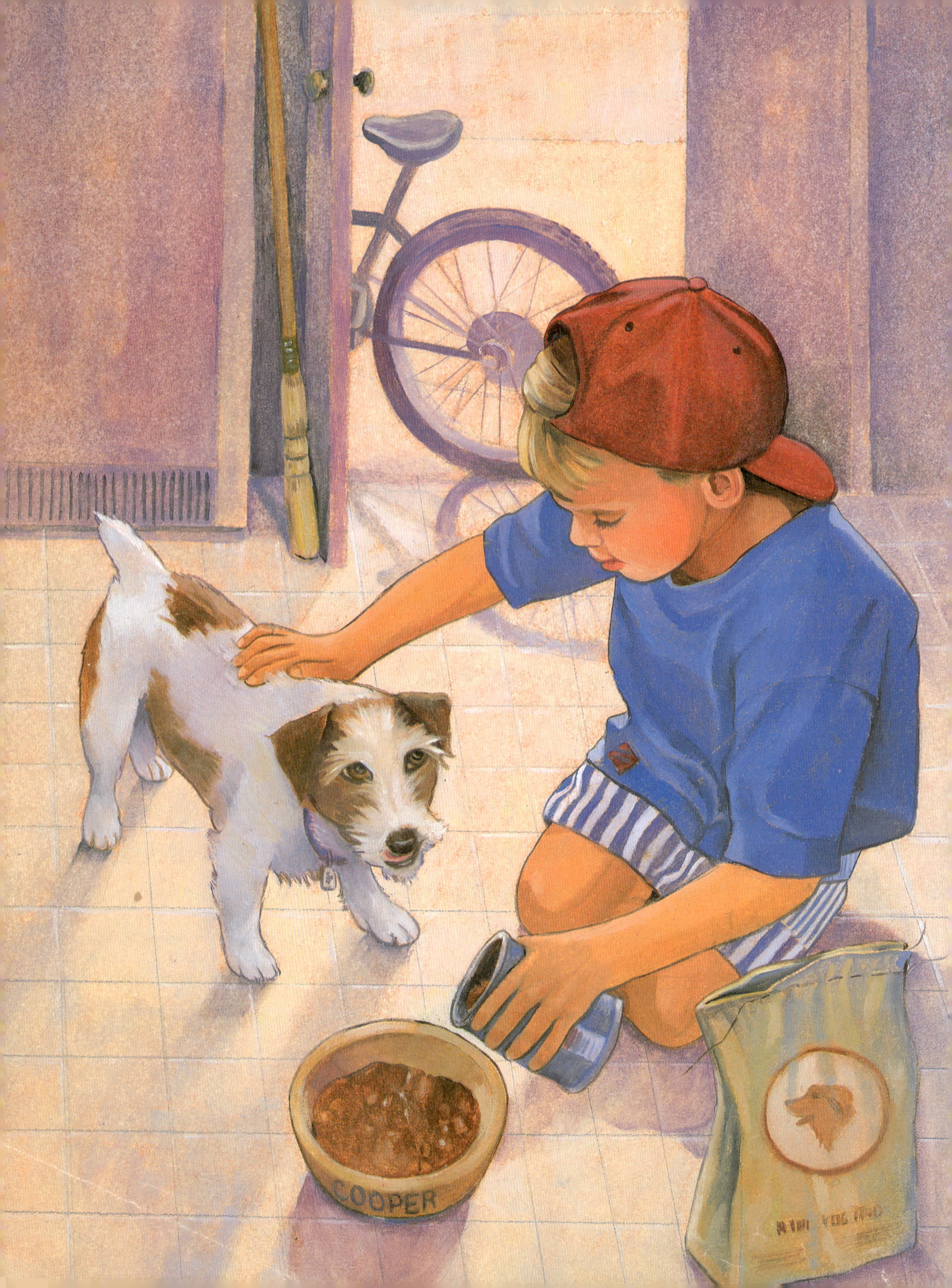
COOPER

Sorry I Lied

"Dad," I hollered, "I'm going to play!"
"Wait!" he said, "Did you feed the dog today?"
I told him yes and ran outside,
hopped on my bike, and started to ride.

But later, when I got home,
there was Cooper, all alone.
His dish was empty,
his eyes looked sad.
I felt very bad.

"Here's your dinner, my skinny friend.
I'm sorry I lied;
I won't do it again."

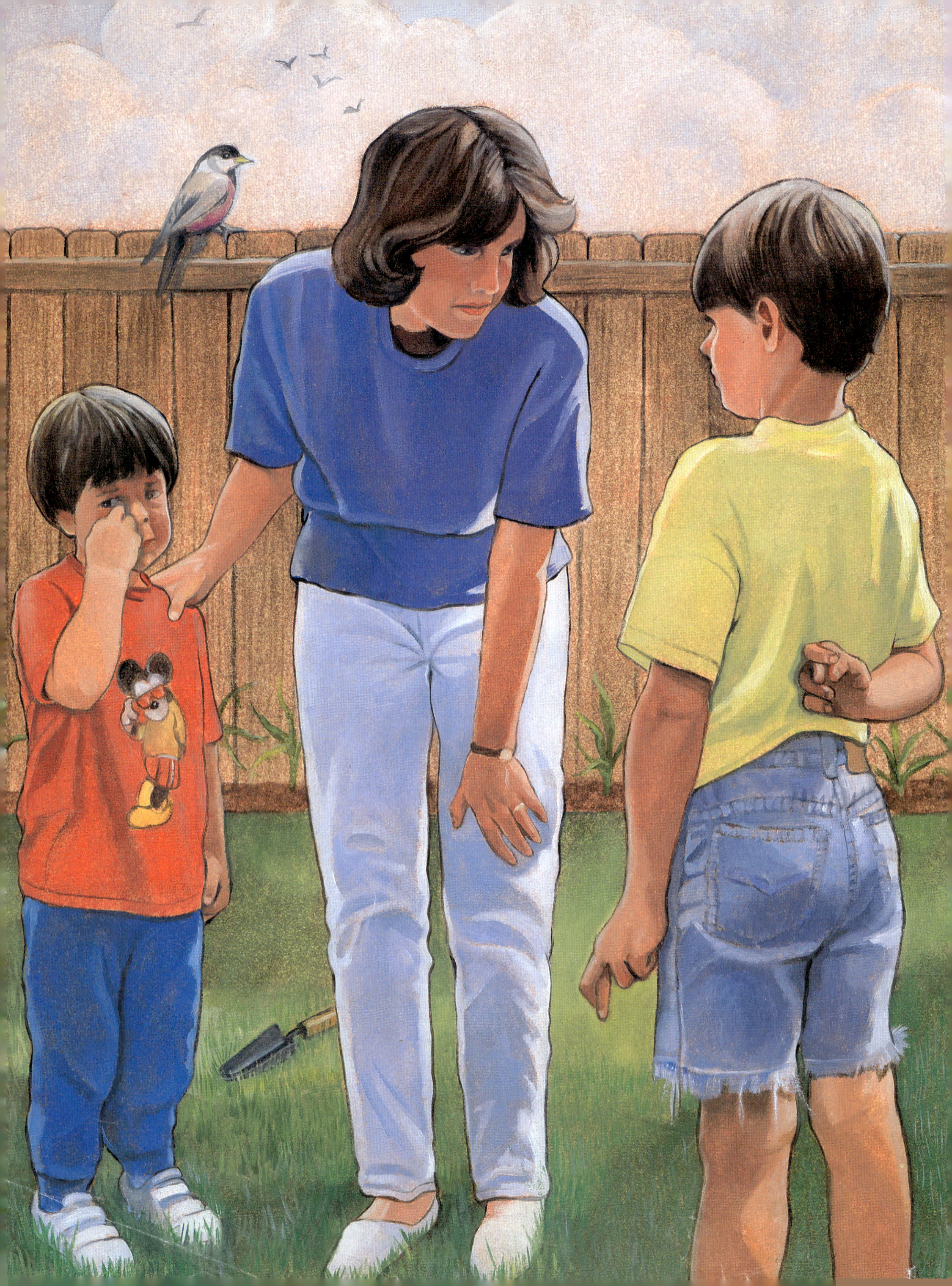

Crossed Fingers

My brother threw a big, fat rock
and gave my head a nasty whack.
"YOW!" I yelled.
Then Mama came. "Who did it?" she asked.
"Not me," said Shane.
"It's not fair," I wanted to announce,
"Crossing fingers doesn't count!"

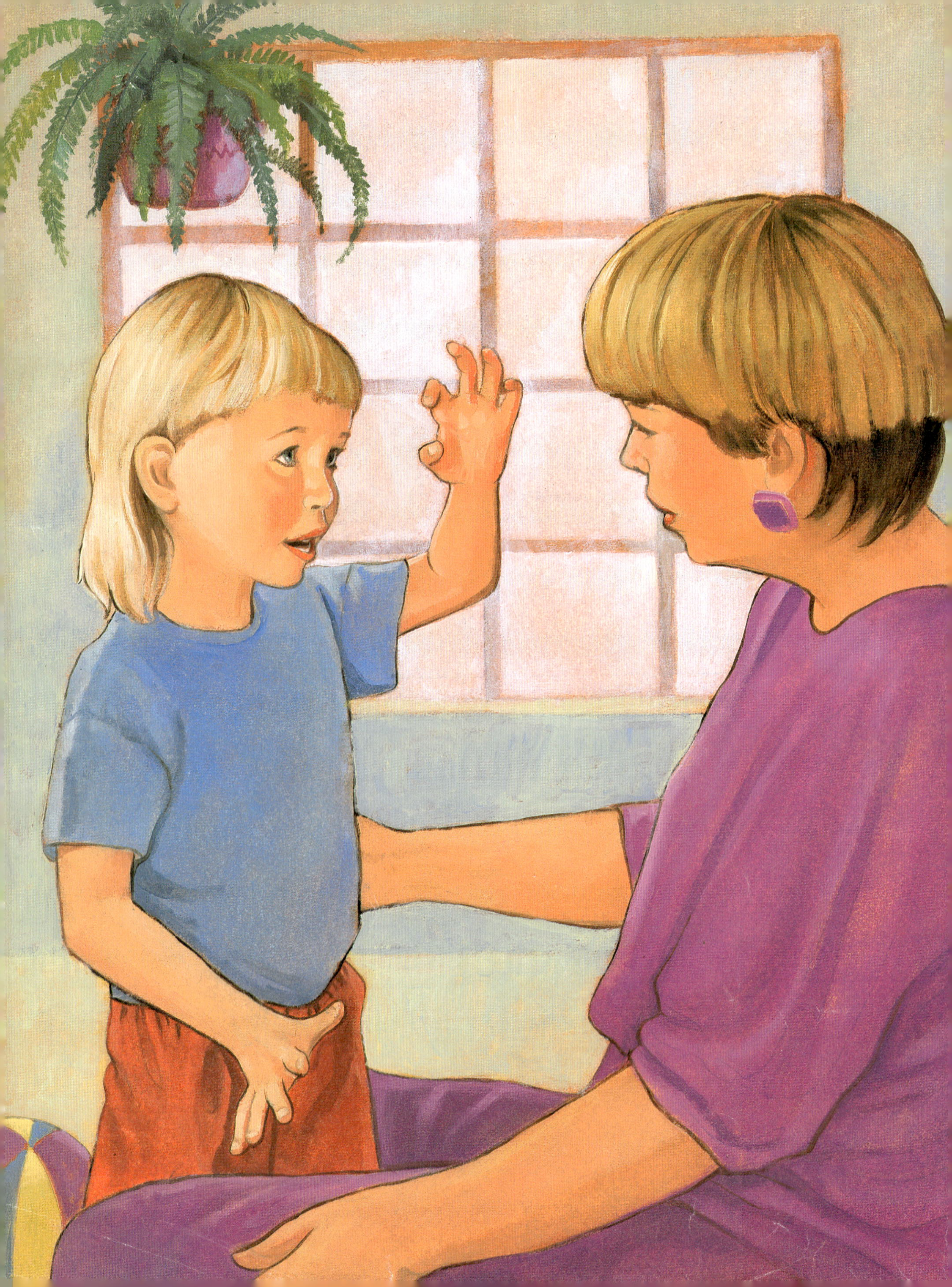

Honest!

I saw a red-striped spider.
Honest, I did!
It was hairy and fat
and *this* big.
You believe me, don't you?
I knew you would.
The best part of always telling the truth
is that people believe you
when they should.